MAKE
WITH YOUR
SMARTPHONE

2023 GUIDE TO SELLING STOCK FOOTAGE

BUILD A SOLID PASSIVE INCOME
WITH THE PHONE IN YOUR POCKET

BY GRAY JONES

FOREWORD BY NOAM KROLL
EDITED BY KYLA JONES

This book was published thanks to free support and training from: TCKPublishing.com

TESTIMONIALS

I honestly never knew that I had a whole revenue stream in the palm of my hands until I read this book! Gray Jones breaks down the stock footage world into easy-to-follow guidelines to lead you to success. I have been taking photos/videos leisurely for years now, and never imagined it could've possibly been lucrative! After reading this book, I feel so much more confident in my skills, knowing I can turn my every day iPhone captures into an income!! Absolute game changer!! Only read if you are ready to make some passive income!

- Vartuhi O. (33) Los Angeles, CA - Director/Producer

Have you ever wondered how in the world Stock Footage works or how individuals make money on sites like Pond5? Well, Gray Jones's new book answers those questions and more. I read straight through it in just a few hours' time 'cuz it was so easy to follow along. The book is filled with great examples, photo samples and stories that really inspire and excite you to want to search for those perfect (and not so perfect) moments in one's life and begin shooting footage from the 4k cell phone in your pocket, upload it to these sites he mentions in the book and start building some passive income. With every chapter, you will find simple step-by-step guides that you will need to potentially change a photo -- into a career! 5 Star Review!

- Hilliard G. (52) West Hollywood, CA - TV/Film Writer, Producer, Podcaster

I know many retired friends who can barely make ends meet, and this would be a perfect way to make some extra income. Gray Jones offers the perfect "problem/solution" answer. This "how to" book is a detailed step-by-step guide, explaining how you can take capitalize on the need for extra income by using - as the author says - what is now most likely in your pocket. The book is extremely well-written in an informal, conversational tone... yet is chock full of important information and useful tips. It is a valuable resource for people of all ages, especially those who are retired.

- Ira H. (75) Sherman Oaks, CA - Professor Speech Communication, retired, Screenwriter, Podcaster

CONTENTS

FOREWORD BY NOAM KROLL

Gray's latest book is an essential read for entrepreneurial filmmakers and creative people of all ages who want to increase their revenue. I've worked for many years as a filmmaker, having produced or directed hundreds of projects to date. If there's one thing I've learned over the years it's the importance of creating multiple revenue streams, both as a means to fund passion projects and find the time to execute them.

Stock footage is a wonderful avenue for any creative to explore in this respect, as many have the potential to make a substantial income using assets they already have or could easily produce. It's pretty amazing that today, using nothing more than the iPhone in your pocket, you can effectively launch a lucrative stock footage business and start generating more cashflow immediately.

The challenge most face is determining what type of material to actually produce, where to sell it, and how to market it to optimize the potential for sales. In this new book, Gray has generously shared his wealth of knowledge on all of the above and more, using his own real world experience and successes in the industry as a guide.

- Noam Kroll, Director
    Website/Blog: noamkroll.com
    Twitter: @noamkroll
    Instagram: @noamkroll
    Facebook: @noamkroll
    YouTube: @Noamkroll

INTRODUCTION

Let's face it—we live in a side hustle culture. Recent stats say that a whopping 49% of Americans in the 18-35 age group have a side hustle, and we spend an average 13 hours/week on it. It's not just young people—41% of ages 36-54 and 27% of 55+ do as well.

Even more shocking: 60% of Americans—more than half—live paycheck to paycheck. The cost of living is high, and for many of us, our day job isn't providing enough income to pay our bills. 58 Million Americans have absolutely nothing saved for retirement, and a shocking 75% don't even think they CAN save enough, even though we all know social security will be inadequate.

What if the escape ladder was in your pocket?

Maybe you're happy with your job and just want some extra cash… or you're having trouble making ends meet. You may be a cinematographer, or perhaps you haven't shot a video in your life. Whether you want to dabble or create a full retirement strategy, I'll show you what you need to do.

Initially, I just started this as a hobby, but now stock footage provides me real passive income to help weather the storms of life and ride out the ebbs and flows of freelance work. I am well on the way to having a six figure income from it and being truly financially free. I'm going to give you all the tools you need to do the same, with zero initial cost (beyond what you paid for this book).

MY STOCK FOOTAGE STORY

Back in 2010, I was editing a TV series that would buy $25,000 of stock footage per episode. The series involved re-enactment of historical events, and much had to be built from scratch using stock footage (crime and unsolved mysteries series tend to be like this).

As often happens on the shows I edit, we were tasked with searching the various stock sites to find clips to fill the holes where we didn't have anything shot by our re-enactment crew. Some was easy to find... scenic shots of Chicago, clouds moving quickly (which shows passage of time), and crowds walking.

However, I would find surprising holes in the stock footage catalogs. Not one shot of the Bronx. Not one shot of an ocean resort town in Mexico. Not one shot of bacon frying! I thought to myself, "I could have easily captured that while I made breakfast this morning." So I did.

I bought a camera and started shooting. Early efforts were disappointing, so I did a ton of research and kept shooting. Pretty soon I had 50, 60, 100 clips... and the sales started happening. It's an exciting feeling, like the "cha-ching" of an eBay sale! But unlike eBay, there is nothing to ship. It's true passive income. Once I plant the seeds, they grow on their own.

I looked everywhere for things to shoot—family trips to the zoo, Niagara Falls, holiday parties, or even my glass kettle boiling water. The sales just kept growing.

As of the time of this writing in 2023, I have single clips that have made over $16,000, single months that I've made $10,000, and my revenue continues to grow (even during years I don't add a single clip to the library). One of my clips is the 64th highest selling 4K clip on Pond5.

Stock footage has opened other doors too… I have been approached several times to shoot directly for a client because of what is in my catalog, and this has led me to all-expenses-paid trips across the US. Most recently, I negotiated a first-look deal with one of the biggest Hollywood studios that they will look first at my footage, before checking anywhere else. As I write this, I am planning a 4 month international shooting trip: you will see my footage in at least a dozen TV series this winter, as well as a commercial for a major TV brand and at least one feature film.

WHY YOU SHOULD READ THIS BOOK

Many people will tell you that stock footage is a saturated market. That is simply not true! I've had some of my best months by far in 2022 and 2023, and my stock footage performed very well even through the ups and downs of the Covid pandemic.

The barrier to entry is lower than ever before! When I got started in 2010, it costed almost $2,000 to get a decent camera that could shoot 1080p. Now you can shoot cinematic 4K with the phone in your pocket.

Let's say that again — you can shoot cinematic 4K with something you carry in your pocket.

So is it just a provocative statement to say you can make six figures with your phone? A gimmick to sell this book? Not at all. You see, there's a saying in photography that "the best camera is the one you've got." I owned a large professional camcorder for many years, but how often did I use it to capture big family moments? Never. Because I never had it with me. Our family moments were captured on low quality point-and-shoot cameras or our rudimentary phones, simply because that's what we had at the moment.

You might own an expensive drone. A cinema camera. But will you have it on a date? What if while driving to the date, you happen to see a house fire, a car accident, or a protest? You now have the ability to catch unexpected moments, newsworthy moments, beautiful shots, in usable quality, with a camera you ALWAYS HAVE WITH YOU.

My biggest enemy is time. My stock footage library could have been much bigger, but I had to wait for down time between jobs and schedule shoot days and trips. I have missed thousands of opportunities to shoot usable stock clips over the years, all because I didn't have my DSLR with me. Now, that has completely changed.

WHAT IF YOU ALREADY OWN BETTER EQUIPMENT?

We will indeed cover more professional ways of shooting, and phone shooters may eventually want to add more professional tools.

Even if you do own better cameras, I urge you to get to know your smartphone and how to milk the best quality it can produce. Don't skip over those sections in this book! Consider it an important tool in your arsenal. We all know by now they've been used to shoot everything from weddings to feature films. Learn how to quickly access it when the moment arises, and get the best quality shooting mode out of it.

Candles I shot while sitting at a holiday party…
and this shot has sold! View at Pond5:
https://tinyurl.com/SFBook-candles

WHY DON'T MORE PEOPLE DO THIS?

You may ask, if this is such an easy way to build passive income, why doesn't everyone do it? I've asked many people, and it boils down to a few things:

1. fear — thinking they won't shoot good enough content,
2. ignorance — they're not aware of the great opportunity,
3. they're precious with their content, or
4. not knowing where to start and how to do it.

I'm often explaining how easy it really is to colleagues and friends (usually when they hear my phone ding with a new sale). One coworker made $1,000 on his first month!

Early on, to help me explain it to people, I gathered my research and put together a blog post. The more I learned, I kept adding to it and refining it. But I found that as I was helping friends through the process, they had a lot of questions that my blog couldn't cover.

I further expanded the material and taught a webinar on it through Moviola Learning. But that still wasn't complete enough.

WHY THIS BOOK, AND WHY NOW?

There have been major shifts in the market that are completely changing the game:

1. 6K and 8K are becoming much more affordable (you can even shoot 8K on some phones),
2. smartphones are now accepted by stock footage sites, and can shoot high quality broadcast codecs like Apple ProRes,
3. vertical video is not only being embraced, but actively being sought, and
4. AI is helping speed up and improve workflows so you can do better titles, descriptions and keywords while spending less time on the process.

Ultimately, I wrote this book because I couldn't find a single resource that adequately explained how to build an effective stock footage library in 2023 and beyond, including these significant new changes in the market.

My favorite stock footage book, "How to Make Money Shooting Stock Footage," by respected shooter James Orlowski (who happens to be the first person I knew who made a 6 figure income from stock footage), is sadly out of print and no longer available online.

When I spoke to James about updating it, he said he just didn't have the time, and now that he's making all the money he needs from his library, he doesn't have any motivation to. Wouldn't it be great to be in that position?

CHAPTER 1: WHAT IS STOCK FOOTAGE?

In this chapter, I'll explain what stock footage is, why it's in demand, who the different buyers are, and how it's always evolving.

STOCK FOOTAGE DEFINED, AND HOW IT IS LICENSED:

Stock footage, or "microstock," is pre-recorded video footage that is licensed for use in films, TV shows, commercials, industrial/educational videos and other forms of media. It can be used to supplement or replace original footage, adding visual interest, context, or information to a project.

Even though you will often hear a person say they "bought" stock footage, that generally means that they licensed it. The same clip can be licensed by an unlimited number of buyers. This is all transparent to you—you plant the seed, and your work is done. After that you just reap the fruit. Each tree keeps producing more and more fruit, with no further intervention from you.

The license is limited by the stock agency's licensing agreement, which includes limits on how the clip may be used (for example, it might be limited to 40,000 views—if you go over that view count, you have to pay more). Often there are different pricing levels for expanded usage.

Stock footage is typically shot by videographers or filmmakers who submit short clips for stock agencies. It often surprises my friends how short these clips need to be—from as little as 3 seconds to 30 seconds, but usually 10 to 20. You would be amazed how many videos you've already shot would sell as stock footage—I estimate that anyone who has owned a smartphone for a few years has at least 100 usable shots already in their phone. You can also use outtakes that weren't used in an edit, older footage you shot with your family or friends, and even archival sources like old family films.

As a matter of fact, that's how stock footage agencies started about 20 years ago! Much of their initial catalogs was built with footage that ended up on the cutting room floor that producers and cinematographers wanted to try to monetize.

WHY IS STOCK FOOTAGE IN DEMAND?

Stock footage is in high demand because it can save time and money for content creators. Rather than filming new footage for every project, stock footage can be cheaply licensed and easily integrated into existing projects. It also allows for more flexibility and creativity, providing access to footage that may not be possible to shoot in-house.

Imagine I need a shot of the San Francisco Bay Bridge. Which is cheaper, licensing one for $79, or sending a crew there to shoot it? Even if I send a crew, I may not get the right shot—on microstock sites, I can choose from a variety of clips.

Bay Bridge at night – view on Pond5:
https://tinyurl.com/SFBook-baybridgenight

From a buying perspective, when I'm looking for a shot, I often don't really care how it looks. If I need shots of a prison fence, a person rubbing a sore knee, or general "scenics" (background scenery of a particular city or location), I will take what I can get.

Don't overthink it! You could stop right now and record your hand rubbing your own knee. Or if you're at the park with your kids or in the line at Starbucks, pull out your phone and find something to shoot. It really is that easy!

Look for color and movement in your daily life!
View this candy shop clip on Pond5:
https://tinyurl.com/SFBook-candy

WHO ARE THE DIFFERENT BUYERS OF STOCK FOOTAGE?

There are many different types of buyers of stock footage, including independent filmmakers, commercial or educational producers, web designers, vloggers, churches, YouTube influencers, marketing agencies, students, or people making videos for their family and friends. It's becoming more and more common for people to edit their own videos to advertise their side hustles or small businesses, and they may build the entire ad with stock footage.

Some buyers may be looking for specific types of footage, such as aerial shots or footage of a particular city, while others may be looking for more generic footage that can be used in a variety of projects (for instance, a birthday background that they could use for multiple birthdays).

How is Stock Footage Evolving?

Stock footage is constantly evolving, with new technology and trends shaping the industry. For example, the increasing popularity of drones has led to a rise in aerial footage, while advancements in camera stabilization have led to more fluid and dynamic shots. Additionally, new types of footage, such as 360-degree video and virtual reality footage, are emerging, providing new opportunities for content creators.

Market Tip – Church Backgrounds

One example—in recent years, many churches have upgraded their audio-visual setup to project lyrics to the songs on big screens. I was tasked with building these for my local church, and we had to buy a ton of long, slow moving nature backgrounds, drone shots, and graphic animations to put behind the lyrics. We couldn't just repeat the same ones, so had to get a wide variety of footage—literally hundreds of clips. That's just one church out of over 400,000 in North America alone. This is a need that didn't exist 5 years ago.

Most stock footage clips are under 30 seconds. If you want to tap into this church market, submit longer, slow moving videos, usually wider nature scenes. There's a 60-second limit on most stock sites, but get as close to that limit as possible. Slow moving motion graphics work great as well.

Tech trends also greatly influence stock footage. Standard definition footage got saturated, but then 1080p opened a new door. Eventually 1080p got saturated, but 4K opened a new door. Currently there are very few 5K+ stock footage clips—if you can shoot these first, you will get sales faster than if you just shoot 4K (though 4K will stay relevant for a very long time, as both broadcast delivery and streaming would have to pay a tremendous amount of money to upgrade their infrastructure for higher resolutions).

Other trends like 360° VR files like with the affordable Insta360 cameras, super slow motion at higher resolution, gimbals, and phones that can shoot cinematic footage have all contributed to drive needs in the microstock catalogs.

VERTICAL VIDEO

What about vertical video? It may have been dreaded by TV editors like me, but vertical video is here to stay. And guess what? There's very little of it yet on the stock sites—literally 0.6% of Pond5's catalog at the time of this writing. That translates into a HUGE gold rush of opportunity! You could have the first vertical shot of a hummingbird, the first vertical shot of a refrigerator, the first vertical... you name it!

In stock footage, the first footage of each type will get more views, more sales, and appears higher in search results, which in turn repeats this cycle.

Before you rush out and shoot only vertical video, though, you have to think from the buyer's perspective. Who will search for vertical video, and what might they be looking for? Vertical video favors close shots of people. Here are some examples:

1. video call with a friend or family member,
2. lifestyle videos like hanging out at a club or having a meal together,
3. playing with your kids, or
4. hanging out at school.

All that said, I can't stress enough how much of an opportunity vertical video represents. Let's put it another way - if you wrote the first ebook on AI, how well do you think it would sell? Pro shooters and landscape mode purists would do well to take heed. And don't forget you can just turn a pro camera 90 degrees to shoot vertically!

Chapter 2: Building Passive Income with Stock Footage, and Other Financial Considerations

In this chapter, we'll define passive income, explain its benefits, and how selling stock footage can be an easy yet powerful source of building passive income.

What is Passive Income, and Why Should I Want it?

Passive income is income that is earned without active involvement or ongoing effort. It is typically earned through investments, real estate rental properties, or other types of businesses that generate income without requiring daily attention. Royalties and residual payments can be examples of this, or affiliate income from Amazon or other retail sites.

There are many benefits to generating passive income, including financial stability, freedom, and flexibility. Passive income provides a reliable source of income that can supplement or even replace traditional income sources, providing greater financial security. Additionally, passive income can provide more freedom and flexibility in terms of work-life balance, allowing you to pursue other interests or hobbies.

In the beginning, you may find it helpful to reinvest the income you earn to help buy better tools, like a tripod, gimbal/stabilizer, lenses, or lights. Alternatively, you can save up for trips to places where you can shoot footage.

Selling stock footage can be an easy yet powerful way to build passive income, because unlike many other types of passive income like real estate or the stock market, there is no investment needed. Once you have created and uploaded your footage to one or more stock agencies, it can be licensed multiple times, providing a source of income without requiring ongoing effort or attention. As you continue to create and upload new footage, your portfolio will grow and diversify, providing even more opportunities for licensing and passive income generation.

How passive is it? I've had whole years that I was too busy to add anything to my catalog, and yet my stock footage income continued like clockwork, even steadily increasing. There are many reasons for this, but the main one is that the more sales and views you have, it rises your footage higher and higher in the search results. Plus, the stock agencies are actively marketing their catalogs... I've even had them use my footage in one of their promotional reels (when stock agencies do this, they provide viewers links to buy the footage — which they did!).

Portfolio Earnings

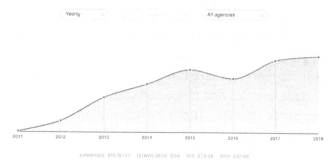

This graph shows my overall earnings from 2011 through part of 2018. As you can see, outside a dip in 2016 (which I believe was due to one agency closing down), my sales have grown very steadily year after year. Some of these years, I barely uploaded any clips, yet it continued to grow. Note that the sampling from 2018 was only part of that year's sales – it ended up significantly higher.

OTHER FINANCIAL & TAX CONSIDERATIONS

You must remember that just like with any other side hustle or home business, you will need to set aside a portion for your taxes. As your stock footage income grows, this will become increasingly important.

On the positive side, there are many other financial benefits to shooting stock footage—you can write off hotels, meals, mileage driven, car purchases, photography books and courses, camera/gear/phone purchases, the computer and software you use to edit the files, your internet service for uploading, and meals on the road. You can even take vacations, and as long as you can prove that you shot stock footage for a significant portion of the time, you can write off many of the trip expenses. The more write-offs you have, the less tax you pay. Of course, you'll need to keep detailed records of your shoots, business mileage, etc, and prorate the write-offs based on what percentage you actually used them in the business. This may also vary from country to country, and change from year to year—be sure to check what kind of home business write-offs you are allowed to take on any given tax year.

This is not a substitute for advice from your accountant, but this is something I highly suggest taking advantage of. It can save you thousands of dollars per year. This year, our tax refund is funding our next 2-month shoot trip!

CHAPTER 3: GETTING STARTED

In this chapter, we're going to look at assessing what's available to us, including considering the pros and cons of phone shooting, the best interchangeable lens cameras if you go that route, and what type of software you'll need.

PERSONAL INVENTORY

The first thing you need to do before rushing out to buy gear is to take an inventory:

1. What equipment is available to you? What are your phones and tablets capable of shooting? Do you have a DSLR, mirrorless camera or camcorder? Tripod? Gimbal? Drone? Lights? What could you borrow?
2. What have you already shot? Look through your photo app and filter it to just see the videos. Can any be repurposed? This includes shots with people, as long as you can get them to sign model releases. One very old clip of our daughter interacting with a peacock when she was young was licensed by a TV show, and has sold multiple times on the stock sites.
3. Do you have older films, audio tapes or video tapes that might have content of historical interest? Even if you can't get model releases, it may be usable as "editorial" footage (more on that later). Check out http://avgearguy.com if you need tapes or films transferred. Pond5 has a great archival section.

4. What props do you have around the home? I have shot and sold water boiling in a kettle, hummingbirds on our balcony, and me & my wife doing various activities like washing hands, coughing, etc.

A simple black or white cloth background can add big production value to your home shoots—buy these cheaply on Amazon. View on Pond5:
https://tinyurl.com/SFBook-cough

PERSONAL INVENTORY CONTINUED...

5. Where do you live? What can you capture around you? You know your town better than any crew who comes to visit.
6. Which friends or family members could be models for you? A shot of a hand picking up an apple will sell better than just a still shot of apples. Shots of people are always in demand (look especially for diversity of race and age). You can get standing releases for people you use regularly (model releases you keep on file so you don't have to get a new one every time).

7. Think outside of the box! A wheelbarrow, wagon, wheelchair, or even a remote controlled car can be used to move the camera, with a little duct tape and ingenuity.
8. Do you have space to create a little home studio? It can be as simple as some poster board and clip lights. There are TONS of YouTube videos on YouTube on DIY film projects. A great place to start is the @FrugalFilmmaker.

There are tons of examples of what you can shoot around the home! View on Pond5:
https://tinyurl.com/SFBook-kettle

Pond5 recommends the iPhone 14 Pro or the Samsung S23 Ultra as a minimum for best phone footage. If you don't have the latest model, you might be able to upgrade at low or no cost. Check with your carrier to see what your options are. And if you are upgrading, you probably want one with a lot of storage.

Pond5 recently put out an article with tips on phone shooting: https://tinyurl.com/P5-PhoneTips

Some general comments on using phones — modern smartphones are marvels of engineering, and have proven adequate for cinematic weddings, music videos, and feature films. But we must also be conscious of the physics of the phone.

On the plus side, the small size and weight of a phone make it incredibly portable. The super-small sensor and wide lens make it very easy to stabilize, and it has a very deep depth of field (the amount of the image that is in focus).

But on the minus side, if you are going for a shallow cinematic depth of field, it is harder to achieve with a phone. You may need to invest in external lenses, and if your camera has multiple lenses, use the longest focal length (the most zoomed in). Also, the tiny sensor isn't as good at absorbing light — that's why phone footage looks amazing outdoors, but can fall apart indoors. As a result, you may want to invest in some lights, or at least be always aware of having as much light as possible.

Ultimately, when you're shooting with the phone in your pocket, it's virtually a zero risk, zero investment, 100% reward situation. But there will come a time that you will wish to up your shooting game, and there are ways you can mitigate risk when you do. Here are some ideas:

1. Wait to buy new gear until you have the earnings to pay for it,
2. Borrow or rent instead of buying,
3. Ask for a phone upgrade, tripod or a gimbal for a birthday or holiday gift,
4. Buy used / refurbished,
5. Use equipment you rented for other shoots before you bring it back.

I will stress again, start with what you have. Once you start having some sales, you can re-invest in an improved interchangeable lens camera and/or support equipment. But you don't have to — I hold that if you are creative and work hard and consistently, you can create a six figure passive income with only the phone in your pocket.

MASTER THE BASICS

I highly suggest doing some homework on photography basics, like aperture, ISO, depth of field, and composition. The phone will do a lot for you, but if you want to attract the most buyers, it helps to have at least a basic skill level.

If you're a self-starter, there are tons of free tutorials on YouTube, as well as photography blogs and websites. If you look on the book website at http://sellstockebook.com, I will provide links to recommended books, most of which I've read.

You might notice that a lot of the books I recommend are for still photography. An aperture is an aperture, whether in a still camera, camcorder, or phone. In my first year of film school, our first assignments in my film production class were with still cameras, because they wanted us to learn the basics of aperture, ISO, shutter speed, depth of field and composition before we got distracted by the movement of the camera. And the good news is that you can get great books on photography and cinematic video at the library or on Kindle Unlimited, instead of buying them.

If you're not a self-starter, local camera stores and community programs and clubs may offer free or inexpensive hands-on in-person courses.

WHEN YOU WANT TO UP YOUR GAME

If you have a budget and really want to go for a pro camera, drone, slider, jib, or other high end equipment, I have some educated recommendations. I don't list too many specific cameras or models here, because it dates a book very quickly. As a result, I have prepared a web page that I will endeavor to keep updated with my latest recommendations. You can find my recommended gear list on this book's website at http://sellstockebook.com.

In general, you should choose the highest resolution your phone or camera allows. The caveat is that resolution isn't everything... codec and bit rate (how much data per second is allotted to store the audio and video file) matter greatly. If you have the ability to record in Apple ProRes, it will be preferred by the stock footage sites and buyers, and choose the highest resolution that will still allow you to shoot in ProRes. If you don't have access to ProRes, choose both the highest resolution and highest quality setting. H265 will record better quality than H264, yet take up less space.

VERY IMPORTANT: phones tend to hunt for exposure and focus, which can cause unwanted shifts. There are many apps that allow you to manually control the settings and lock them in, as well as giving you controls usually found only on DSLR cameras. Pond5 recommends Filmic Pro, Cinema FV-5, and/or ProCam.

OTHER CAMERA OPTIONS

If you're going to buy a dedicated exchangeable lens camera now, it doesn't make sense to buy one that is limited to 4k. At the time of this writing, the Panasonic GH6 (Link https://tinyurl.com/BuyGH6) would be my preferred camera for stock footage — it can shoot 6k, slow motion at high resolution, and can even shoot ProRes in camera, or ProRes RAW with an external recorder like the Atomos Ninja V+. Over the years, the Panasonic GH series has continually been the best for stock footage.

The GH6 is the camera I personally use for 6K stock footage. Being the first to have 6K of any one thing can really help your clip stand out and get early sales, which in turn makes it appear higher in search results.

The first 6K Andean Cock of the Rock on Pond5:
https://tinyurl.com/SFBook-andean

Don't be afraid to buy used! I shot over 14,000 stock footage clips with a Panasonic GH4, and they're still very usable, though you will be limited to 4K. You can get them used for around $450-500 now. Facebook Marketplace tends to be the place for the best deals on used gear like this, though I would also try other listings like OfferUp, Craigslist and eBay.

If you're in a larger city, it may be helpful to rent the gear you need through a service like ShareGrid, LensRentals, or KitSplit. You usually get a full weekend for the price of 1 day, or a week for the price of 3 days, and it's amazing what you can accomplish in a short time if you plan well. If you want to rent from me, my ShareGrid profile is here (though I often have to pause my rentals when I'm away on one of my shoot trips): http://tinyurl.com/RentGray.

If you prefer a different brand like Blackmagic Design, look for a camera that can record at higher resolution than 4k (though a used Pocket Cinema Camera 4K would also be a great budget option, limited to 4K like the GH4 above).

As for lenses, I would start with a standard zoom lens (like the Lumix Pro 12-35mm or Lumix 14-140mm lenses), but eventually you're going to want a super-wide angle lens (like the Lumix 7-14mm). Most stock footage tends to be shot wide, unless you specialize in wildlife or macro photography; in these cases, you will need a long telephoto lens or macro lens. I've used every one of these lenses extensively, and will post all my current recommendations on this book's website at http://sellstockebook.com.

Lenses, tripods, and other support equipment long outlast the camera, and can be bought used to save you money. For lenses, you just need to make sure the lens surface isn't scratched, and that there's no dust or mold inside the lens. If you're using your phone, you may want to invest in a lens protector.

Make sure you save up for Black Friday and similar sales events—I have saved hundreds of dollars on cameras and accessories on these sale days. You can also save by buying the previous model—when a new model comes out, the old model will often go on sale. And if it's been out a while, you can buy refurbished.

Phone shooters: You likely already have the software on your smartphone to edit the videos you shoot with the phone. Similarly, most computers ship with free software for doing simple edits, and you can get free open source software too.

Whether on phone or computer, simple edits are all you need—you just want to trim the in and out point, and in most cases strip out the sound. Don't trim the picture too tightly—you want a bit of "pre-roll" and "post-roll" (a second or two of extra footage before and after the main action) to give flexibility to the buyer who will be using the footage. When possible, use an editor that doesn't recompress the footage to a different format—this degrades the quality, like photocopying a photocopy.

Stock sites generally prefer that except in rare cases, you do not edit multiple clips together. You should also provide raw camera originals without any color grading or effects.

CHAPTER 4: RESEARCHING STOCK FOOTAGE AGENCIES AND FINDING YOUR NICHE

In this chapter, we'll discuss how to research different stock footage agencies' catalogs to discover the best footage to shoot, as well as how to choose a niche or specialty that will help you stand out in the marketplace.

An important general principle to remember: *if it's easy to shoot, there will be lots of it already for sale.* You'll see lots of clouds, flowers and pets, because these are the easiest things to shoot. Unless you have an extremely special shot, I wouldn't go after saturated topics like this.

Most people tend to shoot from eye level. Can you get down low? Up high? Super-close?

Do you have access to special places, like a military base or a school?

RESEARCHING STOCK FOOTAGE AGENCIES

Researching different stock footage agencies' catalogs is a great way to discover what types of footage are in high demand. Start by browsing each agency's website to get a sense of the types of footage they specialize in and the types of footage they're currently promoting. Tip: an empty search will give you the entire catalog. You can then filter the search with things like resolution, frame rate, etc.

Take note of the types of footage that are in high demand (filter by 4K and above to get the newest clips, and sort your search by "Popular"), as well as the gaps in the market that you might be able to fill. Additionally, pay attention to the types of footage that are currently oversaturated at each agency, as you may want to avoid those areas to avoid competition.

Choosing Your Niche(s)

Once you've researched different stock footage agencies and gained a sense of what types of footage are in demand, it's time to choose your niche or specialty. One effective way to do this is to look around you at the tools, location, and people available to you.

For example, if you live near a beach, you might specialize in footage of ocean waves, surfers, or beach landscapes. Or if you have access to a drone, you might specialize in aerial footage of landscapes or cityscapes. What are your hobbies? You might have access to pottery, sports, other types of arts and crafts. The next time you're at your hobby or event, pull out your phone!

By choosing a niche, you'll be able to differentiate yourself from the competition and build a more targeted portfolio of footage that appeals to specific buyers. But don't be afraid to have multiple niches. You can handle this by using Collections—for instance, I have a lot of water footage grouped into a "Water" collection, artistic backgrounds grouped into a "Backgrounds" collection, and planetary animations are grouped into a "Planets" collection. It can become a little harder to describe yourself when you have multiple niches—try to bring them together into your bio in a way that makes sense.

Ocean shots are some of my best sellers! Most have been composited in After Effects using the Red Giant Psunami plugin. View on Pond5: https://tinyurl.com/SFBook-BigMoon

I don't generally recommend this, but it can be helpful in some cases to have a second account. For instance, I have one account called "DrivingFootage" focused on my driving plates company, and then a second account called "GrayJones" for everything else.

Tip: on Pond5, if you want to search for an artist, you can say "artist:" and then their handle. You can also use that combined with other keywords like "artist:grayjones green eye" or "artist:drivingfootage night tunnel".

Chapter 5: Moving the Camera: Techniques and Tools

One of the biggest keys of cinematography is the movement of the camera. The right camera movement can enhance the emotional impact of a scene, create a sense of motion, and guide the viewer's attention—this also makes your clip stand out to buyers.

In this chapter, we will explore some of the different techniques and tools for moving the camera, including tripods, gimbals, sliders, drones, jibs, and cinematic moves. Check out recommended gear for these categories at sellstockebook.com/gear.

Smartphone Considerations

One way that physics are on the side of the phone is that any support equipment can be much smaller, lighter and most importantly cheaper. The newest phones have great internal stabilization, but there are still tools that can help you move the phone in more creative ways.

The first three items mentioned are applicable to both smartphones and conventional cameras; the last three are more rarely used with phones.

FLUID HEAD TRIPOD

The simplest tool in a photographer's or videographer's kit, but also an essential one for smooth pans and tilts, and holding your phone or camera steady. A good tripod will outlast a camera by many years, so don't be afraid to buy used (my wife and I often see these at thrift stores), and make sure you invest in a good one. You can buy an adapter to easily convert between vertical and horizontal shooting (visit the book website for a link), and you want one that has a fluid (smooth) head. Plus search YouTube for other neat tripod tricks!

GIMBALS

A gimbal is a type of floating stabilizer that allows for smooth, fluid movement of the camera. They use motors and sensors to counteract shaking or tilting, which can create a sense of weightlessness and freedom. Gimbals can be handheld or mounted to a drone, vehicle, or other moving object. Both DJI and Insta360 make great inexpensive phone gimbals, that are small enough to fit in a pocket and can be used anywhere. Both DJI and Zhiyun make superb gimbals for bigger cameras.

This would be one of the first investments I would make after a tripod to elevate the quality of your phone or camera videos—phone gimbals are under $200 at the time of this writing. You may also consider buying a gimbal with camera installed, like the DJI Pocket 2. This would allow you a second camera to shoot at the same time, and won't run down your phone battery. I have used a DJI Pocket 2 for quite a bit of stock footage… it's a great "stealth camera" for when a location might frown on people shooting.

I shot a ton of B-roll of San Diego Comic-Con using a DJI Pocket 2 gimbal. View on Pond5:
https://tinyurl.com/SFBook-sdcc

Sliders

Sliders are a simple and versatile tool for adding movement to shots. They consist of a track and carriage that allows the camera to smoothly glide along a set path. Sliders can create a sense of motion or reveal new information within a scene. You will want one that is motorized, and a few of them have the ability to circle around one point to keep your subject in focus while the camera moves.

Sliders can take time to set up, but are essential to create that super slow, smooth cinematic movement. They can also be used for moving timelapses. And for what they add, they're surprisingly affordable! The newest models can even be controlled by your smartphone.

Even a very small slider like a Trexo slider can make a big difference in how interesting and compelling your shot is.

Example of using a slider. View on Pond5:
https://tinyurl.com/SFBook-slider

The next three items are mainly used with dedicated cameras, and rarely with phones.

Drones - Making It Fly

Drones are an increasingly popular tool for capturing aerial shots, or even indoor shots that move in ways that a handheld camera can't. They offer a unique perspective that can create a sense of grandeur and scale. However, they require a skilled operator and may be subject to regulations and restrictions in some areas.

In the United States, you have to study for and pass the Part 107 test to be able to fly a drone commercially. It's extremely difficult to pass without a course, and you'll have to pay the $140 fee all over again if you fail and have to retake it. As a result, I highly suggest paying for a prep course for this that has a pass guarantee.

You may be tempted to skimp on getting the license if you're flying one of the DJI Mini drones that are under the 250g weight limit (these are in the weight category of recreational drones). But be advised that many stock footage sites require that you prove you are licensed before submitting drone footage, and the law says that if you are using them commercially, you need a license. Please note also that this is usually a 2-person affair—one to fly the drone and one to act as an observer, looking for obstacles.

Be aware that there are a ton of drone operators and businesses now. Though you'll see a lot of ads telling you it's hot, this might not be worth the investment because of how saturated the stock agencies are with great drone footage.

But if flying drones really does interest you, I highly recommend considering a full training course. These not only show you how to get the most cinematic shots, but also how to set up a drone business in your area, how to market it, and how to target real estate, roof inspections, and other types of businesses.

You might consider contacting realtors and roof inspectors in your area and offering a 50% off discount on the first job you do for them. Be sure to get testimonials of a job well done, both written and in video form. I also have had great success with small business ads on Craigslist, which only cost $5/month. Another technique that has been very successful for me is to offer a 10% referral fee in exchange for anyone who recommends my services when it results in a paying job.

I have links to recommended drone courses on the book's website, either for just the guaranteed Part 107 training, or an excellent deal on the full bundle of Drone Pro Academy professional drone training videos: sellstockebook.com/gear. If you want to get up to speed and get money shots quickly, I strongly believe that the full video training suite is the way to go.

JIBS

A jib, also known as a crane, is a long arm that can be attached to a tripod or stand. It allows for sweeping, elevated shots that can create a sense of movement and dynamism. However, jibs can be bulky, take time to set up, and are a pain to carry around because of the counterbalances.

In general, gimbals can produce very similar results to jibs when used creatively. However, there's a reason jibs are heavily used in TV shows and films— used correctly, they provide a unique sweeping effect.

CINEMATIC MOVES

Cinematic moves are more complex camera movements that require planning and precision. They can include techniques like the dolly zoom, where the camera moves towards or away from the subject while zooming in or out, or the whip pan, where the camera quickly pans or tilts to create a blur effect. These moves can create a dramatic or surreal effect, but require a skilled operator and planning. Phones generally don't have the type of control necessary for shots like this.

WATCH BEHIND THE SCENES VIDEOS

There are many Instagram accounts that show behind the scenes of photography, TV and movies. I'm constantly inspired by the things I see. Many are not within my reach, but some give me very practical, actionable ideas, and they often show phone cinematography techniques.

A few examples of good Instagram accounts to follow:

- @howwastaken
- @movie.effects.biz
- @camera_pros
- @moviefilmhouse
- @cinematogr

If you find other good ones, shoot me a note on Twitter (@GrayJones) or Instagram (@grahamajones) and I'll include it in the next edition!

IDEA JOURNAL / LOOK BOOK

I highly suggest keeping an idea journal or look book—have a digital note on your phone or computer where you gather samples of techniques you like and want to try, samples of looks you want to do, or any other inspiration that hits you. When I see a behind the scenes video that I want to imitate, I will save a link to it in my idea journal.

MOVE THE SUBJECT TOO

Another tip: don't just move the camera—move what's in the frame too. I had a conversation with the person who built the world's largest stock footage library of food. He told me that when he studied his sales, he realized that shots of human hands interacting with the food sold much higher than beautiful shots of the food, even if the camera was moving.

In other words, if you have a beautiful studio shot of a bowl of oranges, have a person reach into the frame and pick one up, holding it toward the camera. Or a person taking a bite into a fruit or vegetable. Or cutting it open with a knife.

FUN FACT

How valuable is it to have a specialty? The guy above's food library sold for a whopping $71 million.

CHAPTER 6: WHAT TO SHOOT

In this chapter, I'll give you tips and tricks on how to anticipate buyers' needs, build your library most consistently, and generate the most sales with your footage.

ANTICIPATING THE BUYERS' NEEDS

One of the first things you have to train yourself to do is to stop thinking of getting a beautiful shot. The highest selling stock footage sells not because it's pretty, but because it tells a story. The buyer looks at your clip and a metaphor speaks to them. It doesn't hurt if it's a nice shot, *but it's the idea that sells.*

An extension of that is applicable for scenic B-Roll for use in TV & movies. Yes, you want to get beautiful scenery, but it must be indicative of the location. For instance, I was shooting cycling footage at a park in Tucson for a client, and when he saw it, he said "that doesn't look like Tucson. That could be anywhere! Where are the cacti?" So I had to go back to Tucson and make sure to include local fauna and landmarks in what I shot. When you're shooting scenics of your area, be conscious of highlighting things that are representative of what your area is known for. In New Orleans, it would be the French Quarter. In Tucson, it was cacti. In San Francisco we'd better see one of the bridges or the notoriously steep hills.

About 12 years ago, I shot some beautiful slow motion footage of Niagara Falls. To this day, none of it has sold. But a terrible quality, handheld, interlaced, overexposed shot of an alpaca chewing his food has made over $600. Why? Because the alpaca shot has character, and says something. It also might have helped that it has room for ad copy on the right:

Handheld, overexposed, yet made over $600!
View on Pond5: https://tinyurl.com/SFBook-alpaca

Imagine an expressionless woman looking out of a window clutching a coffee cup. This could be used in a myriad of ways: wistfulness, loneliness, being overworked, being unemployed, being single... or just a woman who loves her coffee.

WATCH TV FOR HOMEWORK? COUNT ME IN!

One of the best ways to research what sells is to pay attention when you're watching movies and television shows (both reality and scripted TV) as well commercials and other types of ads (like on YouTube and Instagram). What shots are clearly stock footage? And what kind of footage are they using? Try to identify the scenics and establishing shots. Ask why they might have picked those ones. What time of day are they? How did they move the camera?

CASE STUDY: STOCK CONTRIBUTOR JAMES ORLOWSKI

James Orlowski is a master at speaking in metaphors. Take a look at his library on Pond5, and you'll see what I mean: https://tinyurl.com/P5-ODesigns

Click to search based on "Popular" to see his highest selling clips. Some clips I notice:

Gas pump: how many times did I fill my car with gas, and never thought to tape the numbers going up! This is a great metaphor for gas prices, inflation, financial woes, and the economy in general.

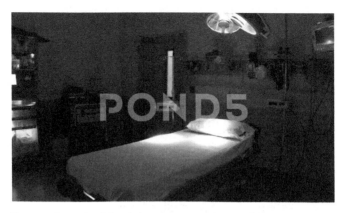

Empty hospital bed: how many times do I wait 10-20 minutes for my doctor... I could shoot a shot like that while I'm waiting! And there are many uses for a shot like that—bed shortages, a death, nurse shortages, a background for general health/hospital titles.

Putting the closed sign in the window... that looks like a simple laser printed piece of paper. How easy would that be to shoot! And yet it says so much — businesses closing due to Covid, staff shortages, a bad economy. James has many other signs like this — "Help Wanted," "Closed Due to Covid-19," etc.

Getting a box from the doorstep, or package theft from the same doorstep. Super easy to shoot, but many uses!

Worried couple crouched over a computer and looking at bills. Think of how this might be used!

Car slipping in snow. Any shots that express challenges of weather sell very well. If there is an extreme weather event, try to capture it! Safely, of course.

Keep in mind these are the highest selling clips from someone who built a 6-figure yearly passive income and never has to work another day in his life! Take some time to study his catalog and learn how he expresses metaphors through very simple shots. Try to ask yourself, what "could" this shot say? As you research other subjects on the stock footage site, ask these same types of questions. Then, look at what you have the ability to shoot. Try to come up with similar ideas on how to bring concepts to life.

VERY IMPORTANT: *an empty hospital bed won't just sell itself. It is crucial that the title, description and keywords and even collections work together to help the buyer find that shot.* We'll learn more about this a little later, and you may want to have another look at James's catalog when you're armed with that information (look how he describes his clips).

Another tip: several of the stock agencies have "what to shoot" resources available to their contributors.

SHUTTERSTOCK: I highly suggest signing up for Shutterstock's excellent contributor email newsletter (no account required). These tell you every month what trends they anticipate, what requests they are getting from buyers, and other helpful articles. Find it here: shutterstock.com/blog/. Even if you don't upload to Shutterstock, sign up for this one.

POND5: Pond5 has a contributor portal at contributor.pond5.com that acts the same way. There are tons of helpful resource pages on what to create, data and trends, tips on building your business, and a forum where you can interact with other contributors. You can find out which are the best selling clips in the past month, trending keyword searches, median sales at different resolutions, and many detailed articles on aspects of growing your business, attracting leads, using social media, etc. Please note that some but not all is accessible without a contributor account.

ADOBE: Adobe has an Artist Hub (contributor account required), which has similar resources to Pond5, but also includes courses on learning everything from the Adobe tools, to lighting techniques, to how to craft effective titles and keywords. Of special note is "Calls for Content" where they are specifically asking for more of something. *Guess what they're asking for in May 2023? More vertical video!*

60P, 30P or 24P?

That is the question! The frame rate has been hotly debated on agency forums, and the general consensus is that if you, like me, intend for your footage to be used in the TV & film industry, you want to shoot at 24P. If the clips will be primarily for online distribution, on sites like YouTube, then you want to shoot at 30P. Sports-related material or anything that may need to be slowed down can be shot at 60P.

BUILDING YOUR LIBRARY CONSISTENTLY

As we continue to try to get into the mind of the buyer, let's think of the various ways they can find footage. Many will search based on what's most popular. That you have to earn over time. But many will search based on what's newest and freshest. They don't want clips that everyone's seen before.

If you take a Saturday and upload 40 clips, and then don't upload again until the next Saturday, you only get a single chance in the week to be at the top of the "Newest" search. If instead you upload 5 a day, that means that at least once every day your clips will be on the top of the Newest searches. If a buyer sees one of your clips and likes it, they are very likely to click on it and see what else you have.

That's why it's so important to have a good profile picture, descriptive bio telling what kind of footage you focus on, and an eye-catching header. You may get one chance with this buyer, and you want to create a fan who will bookmark your page and come back later.

My suggestion on time management—when you have a larger block of time like on the weekend, use that either to shoot new footage, or hunt through previously shot footage, editing and gathering elements into a "ready to upload" folder. Then parse those out for each day of the upcoming week and allow a few minutes each day to do the keywords, titles and descriptions and submit a few clips for review.

I also am a firm believer in setting written goals. Figure out how many clips you can reasonably upload in a week, and then set a goal for the year, and make it happen! James Orlowski was able to retire on a library of about 6,200 clips. If you uploaded just 9 clips a day, you could hit that goal in under 2 years! And that would be only spending half an hour per day... about a quarter of the amount of time of the average side-hustle, yet on the path to building a six figure fully passive income within 2 years.

MORE IDEAS ON WHAT TO SHOOT

And remember to think ahead to holidays and other events like graduations, bar mitzvahs, birthdays, engagements, bridal showers, etc. Have a look at the calendar, and make sure to upload related content as far ahead of the regular holidays as possible. Keep in mind the Christmas music starts playing in the malls on November 1st... which means that any Christmas ads were edited in October. And at the very least, shoot during the holiday or event for use the following year.

Make sure to pull out your phone to capture representative parts of the holiday... putting up Christmas lights outside, laying out the Halloween decorations, giving out candy (try suckers or other candies that have no visible logos), homemade costumes, holiday ornaments without trademarks, pulling the turkey or pie out of the oven, scooping ice cream (no logo visible), cutting the ham, etc. Think of close shots, medium shots and wide shots. Just be sure to get releases for any people appearing (for kids in costumes, I would get releases even if you can't see their face).

Do you like animals? There's lots you can shoot at the zoo or in your area. We love shooting hummingbirds coming to the bird feeder on our balcony. We've even had a major TV brand contact us about using some of our hummingbird footage in a commercial.

Coming to an LG commercial near you! Browse on Pond5: https://tinyurl.com/SFBook-hummingbird

What topics are hot right now? A quick daily scan of the headlines or social networks should tell you what people are talking about. Think about James Orlowski, how he expressed rising gas prices, worker shortages, etc. How will you metaphorically represent the issues on the news? A simple example: try videotaping a computer screen while you type the topic as a search term into Google (close-up so you don't see the Google logo).

Google search example without showing logo— browse on Pond5: *https://tinyurl.com/SFBook-search*

You can also create a home studio very easily to shoot things like fruit, vegetables, meals, drinks being poured, etc. Remember I got into this because there wasn't a shot of bacon frying on any of the stock footage sites. What other things around the home could you shoot?

One extremely common use for stock footage is as a background for text. I often will frame a shot with a relatively blank area, which will allow the buyer room to add graphics or text, or design motion graphics for this purpose. When I do this, I make it clear in the title, description and keywords that this was done intentionally for this purpose.

This doesn't affect everything you shoot, but you might want to keep this in mind when capturing a scene or motion graphic you think could work as a background. Backgrounds are usually priced in the bottom tier but will make up for it in volume.

One of my earliest stock shots, of a sneezing lion—overexposed, shot with consumer camcorder, but has sold thanks to the text area on the right. Was probably used in allergy commercials.
View on Pond5: https://tinyurl.com/SFBook-lion

Our daughter is an avid Dungeons and Dragons player and dungeon master, and I knew the D&D movie was coming out in a few months. It was sure to be on people's minds way more than usual. So we borrowed a number of D&D dice from her, and I rigged up a lazy Susan with a mini-dolly powering a slow rotation, and recorded a bunch of dice rolls with our GH6.

Slow motion D20 dice roll—View on Pond5:
tinyurl.com/SFBook-D20

Pond5 also anticipated the trend with the movie, and they released a blog post highlighting their D&D footage: tinyurl.com/P5-DD-Blog.

For this blog post, they edited together a promo video... which used our dice rolls no less than 6 times! View here: tinyurl.com/P5-DD-Promo.

Whenever Pond5 releases a blog/promo like this, they will also provide a page showing what footage they used, so buyers will have an easy way to buy it: tinyurl.com/P5-DD-Clips.

And buy they did! We have already had multiple sales of our dice rolls in the few weeks since the movie and promo came out.

What trends do you foresee in the coming months? This kind of thing won't happen for every movie, but are there any big movies or events coming up that you think might prompt a need for unique footage?

CHAPTER 7: STILLS, CGI / EFFECTS, GRAPHIC TEMPLATES, 3D

In this chapter, we'll discuss still photography and computer-generated backgrounds, CGI, effects, 3D models/animation and graphic templates.

STILLS

Out of the things we'll discuss in this chapter, stills are the only thing that can currently be done on a phone. Sadly, still photos are an extremely saturated market, as great cameras have been around for a long time and there haven't been as many rapid changes in the market. But some photos will still sell, especially if you have a niche specialty, really great eye, or access to exclusive situations—like military or political events. As this is a book on stock footage, not stills, I recommend doing a search for a book dedicated to this subject that is recent and well-reviewed.

CGI, EFFECTS, BACKGROUNDS & 3D

One of the things I do in my down time between jobs is watch a ton of free tutorials to refresh my compositing and 3D skills, and then just spend time "playing" at the computer. As a result, I've been able to develop a niche specially in CGI and moving backgrounds. Some of my highest selling clips have been built this way, in a few minutes or hours at the computer.

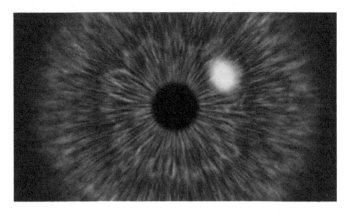

The money shot! This took me about 2-3 hours at the computer and has earned enough to buy a modest new car. It's the 64th top selling 4K clip on Pond5. Check it out: https://tinyurl.com/SFBook-blueeye

These don't have to be complicated CGI shots like the above. As I experiment on the computer, a lot of what I create end up as just simple slow-moving backgrounds for text. You generally price these at the lowest pricing level. They don't sell that often, but you can make up for it in volume.

This background only took a few minutes on the computer, and has made over $200! I will usually render two to four color versions, often just by shifting the hue-saturation control in After Effects. View on Pond5: https://tinyurl.com/SFBook-GreenAura

Did you know that most of the effects of the Oscar-winning movie "Everything Everywhere All at Once" were done by people with no formal training, who just learned by following online tutorials? That's how easy it can be.

You can use 3D apps to render out animations, and you can also sell 3D models as stock. If you're good at 3D modeling, these can be made very quickly. I would spend a lot of time researching what models are the most popular, and how saturated the various topic areas are. For instance, do you see office related 3D models selling the most? Find a list of common office items on the web, and search to see if there are any that are not well represented at the stock agency. Also check the agency shoot briefs, like this "3D models" data & trends page in the Pond5 contributor portal: https://tinyurl.com/P5-3DBrief.

Modeled after a Disneyland ride (Space Mountain) and rendered in a few hours! View at Pond5:
https://tinyurl.com/SFBook-jupiter

If you have a PC (or Intel Mac with Parallels), you may want to try out iClone and Character Creator — you can create characters and other elements that you can then sell on their marketplace.

An example of an iClone animation that I made early in the pandemic. View on Pond5:
https://tinyurl.com/SFBook-anim1

And don't forget different languages... when I generate "Merry Christmas" and other holiday graphics I make sure to do them in several other main languages as well as a blank (textless) version too.

GRAPHIC TEMPLATES

Another lucrative area is creating graphic templates for After Effects and other Adobe apps. There are great tutorials online on how to build these, and new ones are always in demand. Envato is the most well-known marketplace for these, but they pay a relatively low commission. As an alternative, you can also sell them through Adobe and Pond5. If you're non-exclusive at Pond5, I would absolutely upload them to Envato Market, because the high volume should make up for the low commission.

THINK OF THE BUYER FIRST

The principles with 3D models and animations, CGI, backgrounds and graphic templates are very similar to how you approach footage with your phone: you must consider the buyer first. What might they be looking for and how will they be looking for it? A "pretty" CGI shot won't sell any better than a pretty drone shot if it doesn't say anything to the buyer.

CHAPTER 8: SOUND EFFECTS AND MUSIC

Do you fancy yourself a foley artist or a music maestro? Sound and music are handled much the same way as video clips. though some stock footage agencies like Pond5 will sell it, and others won't.

FOLEY / SOUND EFFECTS

If you're interested in creating sound effects, I highly suggest investing in Ric Viers's excellent Sound Effects Bible, available here: https://amzn.to/3VfloBj

You can record some sounds with your phone, but it will be far better to get a dedicated recorder (like one from Zoom or TASCAM), and a good microphone. The book above will tell you all about it.

MUSIC

Writing and recording music is beyond the scope of this book. However, if you have some music that you've written that you haven't licensed anywhere else, you may consider making it available for sale at Pond5 or one of the other sites.

CHAPTER 9: PRICING STRATEGIES

In this chapter, we'll discuss the best ways to price your clips to maximize views, sales, and revenue.

PRICING STRATEGIES

We delve once more into the mind of the buyer… A large number of buyers are working on a fixed budget: they will often search by lowest price then buy the best clip they can afford. There are 2 main ways to take advantage of this:

1. Temporarily lower the price of your entire catalog to get views and sales, which will then make your clips appear higher in "Popular" searches. I will usually set a time frame for this like 1 month, and then raise the prices back to normal ($79-$89 is a good default price for 4K clips). I will sometimes do this when I notice sales taper off, as a way of giving a shot in the arm.
2. Pick a small number of your clips, perhaps the ones you're not as proud of, to permanently price low. These will attract buyers to your catalog, and hopefully keep them coming back for higher priced clips later.

DO NOT CHASE THE BOTTOM

Many new stock shooters will try to imitate Walmart and always price their clips as low as is allowed by the site. In my experience this does *not* lead to a great increase in sales, and you will cut your revenue considerably. *Don't forget the concept of perceived value—when an item is priced higher, a buyer perceives it as having greater value.* Chasing the bottom hurts the whole market because it drives everyone else's prices down.

FREE CLIP PROMOTIONS

Should you opt in to "free clip" promotions? Absolutely yes. I wouldn't necessarily opt in for your highest value footage (for instance high priced military footage), but I would pick a few clips you can assign for these promotions. The stock agency will promote the free clips on their email blasts to hundreds of thousands of buyers. That free clip has now become free advertising of your catalog. Plus, it will get a ton of views and $0 "purchases" that will make it appear higher in searches.

SUBSCRIPTION SALES AND CREDIT PACKS

Should you opt into subscription sales or credit pack purchases? *Under no circumstances!* Not unless you want your clips selling for pennies!

In general, almost all my regular footage is priced at $79, and driving plates at $179. Some are priced lower ($69 or $59) if I think it's not as appealing to buyers. You might want to categorize your footage with tiers... lowest tier intended as bargains, middle tier at $79, and then premium tier at $99 or higher. Always price at the 9's—psychology says that $69 looks a lot cheaper than $70.

Some footage categories that I would price in the lowest tier are general scenics and backgrounds. These are in high demand, but buyers want to buy these categories cheaply. Make sure to have a good variety and keyword them well, and you should be able to make up for it in volume.

If you have very special footage, like shot on a RED, in studio, or with an extreme slow motion camera, you can price it a lot higher, like $299-499 per download. Military footage, or editorial footage where you had special access to a celebrity or major political event, can be priced as high as $999.

You do want to tweak your prices over time, but I wouldn't read into day to day or month to month fluctuations. There are natural seasons and constant ebbs and flows in stock footage. I may have no sales for two weeks, and then 7-8 sales on a single day. I can have a super-slow month followed by my best month ever. If you have a shot that is selling like crazy, try raising its price a little. If you do, keep an eye on that clip for a little while afterward: if you raise the price too much, it could kill the sales.

CHAPTER 10: STOCK FOOTAGE LICENSING, RELEASES, EDITORIAL FOOTAGE AND LEGAL CONSIDERATIONS

In this chapter we'll discuss legalities, intellectual content, trademarks, model and property releases, and editorial footage, as well as notes to the curator.

LEGALITIES & INTELLECTUAL CONTENT

Even stock agencies aren't above theft! One in particular is notorious for outright stealing content and selling it as if it's theirs. I won't mention them by name, but they did something similar to me. You won't see me promoting them in this book.

In general, though, the main stock agencies (Pond5, Shutterstock, Adobe, 123RF, and many others) are trustworthy, and are built from the ground up to protect your intellectual content.

You won't have to think too much about the licensing part of it, except to know that the agency will provide a limited license to use your footage in a set way, for a set audience. You may get more money down the road called an "Extended sale" if the buyer pays to broaden the scope of the license.

For instance, I purchased the still shot for the cover of this book from Pond5. Because I only planned to release this as a Kindle eBook with a small print run, I purchased it at a low price. But if my printed book sales take off, I will need to purchase an extended license from Pond5 (which will cost 50x as much). Even that license is capped at a certain number of sales. If I exceed that number, I will need to upgrade the license yet again.

Trademarks, and Model / Property Releases

You cannot use any footage that infringes on someone else's copyright. This includes any trademarks like logos on clothing, signs, houses where the number is visible or the house shape is recognizable, artwork and sculptures, full buildings where the architecture is unmistakable, zoo animals that are well known, and many other such situations.

Pay attention to what you can hear as well: there may be copyrighted music playing, or recognizable voices. In general, you should strip the sound of the clips you submit. That being said, there may be situations where you want to include the sound (eg. a campfire crackling). When you do intend to use sound, be vigilant that there is not music playing and that no one is talking nearby.

In TV & film, we will often "Greek" a location—this means taping over any logos, pulling artwork down from walls, replacing clothing that has logos, etc. It is *far* easier to do this before you shoot than afterward in post-production.

Getting Model and Property Releases

The way around these restrictions is to secure model and property releases. You can download blanks at any of the stock footage sites. There are also phone/tablet apps you can use to create them digitally.

If you have a property release from the owner of a house (not the rental tenant), you can shoot that house as much as you like as long as you upload and attach that release to every clip shot around that house. I would still avoid shooting the house number.

Any recognizable person needs a signed model release—that's why you will often see people walking away from the camera or out of focus on TV shows. Please keep in mind that you will need a model release for yourself as well, as you will likely be in many of your own shots.

Always have some printed releases with you or the app ready. You'd be surprised how many people would be happy to let you shoot footage of them, after you explain what it's for. For actors and models, it's also common to work out a revenue sharing agreement—for instance, in exchange for appearing in your footage, you give them 20% of all sales of those clips. You can also barter and offer to do an acting reel for them instead. Similarly, if you want to get booth footage at a convention like Comic-Con you may be able to barter shooting promo footage for the booth in exchange for them signing a release for you to sell the footage. Be *very* sure that you get a signed property release for any artwork in the booth as well as model releases for any people in the shots whose faces are recognizable.

Another way around these things is just to avoid the recognizable elements. Technically when I'm shooting in a zoo for any commercial reason I should get permission from the zoo—they might do that for a student production but are unlikely to grant it for stock footage. But as long as I shoot in a way that the zoo is not recognizable, I can submit the footage I shoot. And again, you can shoot people's feet, or shoot people walking or riding away from you, and you won't need releases for them.

A note for cars and other vehicles—you can shoot vehicles passing you, coming toward you, or going away from you, but never focus the camera on the logo, name of the vehicle, or the license plate.

EDITORIAL FOOTAGE

There are special rules for news stations, journalists, and other such buyers that allow them to use footage with recognizable trademarks, even without releases. You can shoot this type of footage ignoring the rules above, but be aware it must be tagged as "for editorial use only" so buyers know what it's appropriate for. Pond5 will assess this as part of the approval process of the clip. In other words, it's not something you control. Other sites will ask you to select this when you are submitting the clip.

Interestingly, there may be cases where such editorial footage is indeed used for commercial purposes. When this happens, this is all transparent to you. The stock footage agency will work out all the licensing directly with the buyer. In many cases, this will mean an extended license and you will get an additional payment.

This shot of flooding in Toronto was marked as editorial because of the license plates. But I've still sold several of them! Severe weather always sells. View on Pond5: https://tinyurl.com/SFBook-storm

The stock sites used to have a much higher rejection rate for editorial footage, but lately they've decided to embrace it. As a result, I would say go ahead and shoot street festivals, parades, picket lines, conventions, and other such events that have tons of logos, trademarks and recognizable people, if they are newsworthy. Just be careful to indicate that it is "for editorial use only" on sites where you need to note it manually.

Some editorial footage is timely—for instance, you witness a house fire, brush fire, tornado, or car accident. Alternatively, you get footage of the first day of a convention and you want it available for sale as soon as possible for news stations that might be covering those events. It is very rare for me to have a special note to the curator, but in these cases I absolutely do. I tell them the urgent nature of the footage, and request that it be processed quickly. They usually will.

CHAPTER 11: SELECTING AND PREPARING FOOTAGE FOR SALE

Depending on your workflow, one of the most challenging parts of the process can be selecting which clips and which parts of the clips to sell. In this chapter, we'll talk about strategies for selecting, organizing, naming clips, and also the importance of having good quality hard drives and a backup system.

GOING THROUGH YOUR CAPTURED FOOTAGE

We already discussed the editing process above in the Software section. But how do you know which shots are good enough to sell? Obviously, they must be properly exposed, in focus, and not shaky. When in doubt, just upload it. I've had stuff sell that I never thought would be of interest.

One exception is variations. If you have 3 very similar shots, try to pick the one that is the strongest. That's not to say you shouldn't have any variations— just that the variations should be different enough to make them worth uploading. For instance, my blue eye clip is my best seller, but I also decided to do hazel, brown and green eyes too. These didn't make as much, but they did earn $2,400 between them.

Another factor—you want to pick shots that get to the meat of the action quickly. You allow for a second or two of preroll, but then the interesting part of the shot should happen almost immediately after that. Buyers won't wait 10 seconds into the shot to get to the action. They'll play for 3-4 seconds and move on if it doesn't get to something interesting.

Something that took me a very long time to learn—do *not* be a perfectionist. You must learn to make a quick decision and move on. Don't be precious with your material; you can always find or shoot more.

ORGANIZING AND NAMING YOUR CLIPS

As you go through your existing footage, it is very important to develop a naming and organizing system early. If you plan to build a 6-figure passive income, this may mean 6,000-12,000 shots. These will need to be named and well organized.

Here are the steps I follow when sorting my footage. Before I begin, I create 4 folders: 1) "To Edit," 2) "Edited to Upload," 3) "Uploaded," and 4) "Back Burner." Then I sort using the following criteria:

1. Any that I consider high priority (the ones I really feel will sell) are placed in the "To Edit" folder.
2. Any that I consider lower priority but still worth uploading at some point (for example, lower resolution) I place in the "Back Burner" folder.
3. As I go through the "To Edit" folder to trim them, I first create a unique number prefix (if the file was IMG_0335 I might call it 0012_Santa Monica ocean waves slow_IMG_0335). I like to have the original file name in the name in case I need to find the raw original later. As I trim them, these get exported into an "Edited to Upload" folder.

4. Clips that have been uploaded and submitted to the stock agency are then moved into my "Uploaded" folder.
5. As your library grows, it may be helpful to group your previously uploaded clips by year.

I highly suggest building a master spreadsheet in Google Sheets, Apple Numbers or Microsoft Excel. That will make it much easier to:

1. track your clips,
2. copy and paste common information like keywords between similar clips,
3. facilitate copying information into the different agencies' submission forms, and
4. prevent errors. I also create a column for Submitted Yes/No and Approved Yes/No for each of the agencies.

All hard drives fail. I have lost an entire solid week of work when a brand new hard drive died. Phones break. Footage gets corrupted. I've seen a client spend $1800 on a film transfer and lose it all when the hard drive went down.

You may be creating a library that will make you a million dollars over the next 10 years. You *must* invest in good quality hard drives and make backups. Enterprise drives, like the ones in LaCie Professional D2 drives, fail 1000 times less than normal drives. In layman's terms, 1000 normal drives will fail before one of those will. So is it worth paying an extra $100 for that security? Absolutely yes. You'll make it back in a couple of stock footage sales.

Head on to the next chapter to learn one of the most important parts of the process, how to describe and title your clips, and generate keywords that help buyers find your clip in the sea of other clips.

CHAPTER 12: HOW TO USE AI AND OTHER STRATEGIES FOR KEYWORDING, DESCRIPTIVE TITLES AND DESCRIPTIONS

In this chapter, we'll discuss the importance of keywording, descriptive titles, and descriptions in selling stock footage. We'll also define SEO (Search Engine Optimization) and how it relates to the titles, descriptions, and keywords. Finally, we'll discuss how to use AI to help us find the best keywords and descriptions.

WHY ARE KEYWORDING AND DESCRIPTIVE TITLES AND DESCRIPTIONS IMPORTANT?

Keywords, descriptive titles and descriptions are essential in selling stock footage because they are the only way that the buyer can actually find your footage in the sea of other clips on the agency's site. Buyers use keywords to find the footage they need, and without proper keywording and descriptions, your footage may not appear in search results, which reduces its visibility and potential for sales.

TIPS FOR EFFECTIVE KEYWORDING, TITLES, AND DESCRIPTIONS

1. **Research keywords:** Research the keywords and phrases that buyers are using to search for footage in your niche. The Google keyword tool can be helpful, and look for popular footage of the same type, and see

how it is described. Use these keywords in your titles, descriptions, and keywords to improve visibility and relevance.

2. **Be specific:** Use specific keywords and phrases that accurately describe the content of your footage. Avoid generic or broad terms that could apply to a wide range of footage (though you should include things like day/night, color, and people vs no people, as buyers will search based on these things).

3. **Think in metaphors:** After expressing the obvious, look for other meanings and emotions the buyer could see in the shot. Try to think of all ways the buyer might search to find it.

4. **Use long-tail keywords sparingly:** Long-tail keywords are more specific phrases of several words that may have lower search volumes but can lead to more targeted traffic and sales. Only use these when the specific meaning is important to your shot— e.g. "squirrel dancing with a hat." Squirrel, dancing, and hat all need to be together to properly understand what this shot is about.

5. **Keep it concise:** Keep titles and descriptions concise and to the point, providing enough information to accurately describe the footage but avoiding unnecessary information or fluff.

6. **Be descriptive:** Use descriptive language to help buyers envision how the footage could be used in their project. Describe the mood,

emotion, setting, and subject matter of the footage to help it stand out. I will often add "Could be used for..." to make sure they understand several possible uses for the clip.

IMPORTANT NOTE ON ETIQUETTE

It is greatly frowned upon to directly plagiarize another contributor's titles, description, and even their keywords. You can imitate them, but always put them in your own words, and add your own flair. Don't copy every keyword, and try to add your own different ones.

WHAT IS SEO AND HOW DOES IT RELATE TO TITLES, DESCRIPTIONS, AND KEYWORDS?

SEO (Search Engine Optimization) is the practice of optimizing your content to rank higher in search engine results. For stock footage, SEO involves optimizing your titles, descriptions, and keywords to improve visibility and relevance in search results. By researching and using relevant keywords, writing descriptive titles and descriptions that include these keywords, you can improve your footage's SEO and increase the chances that it will be seen by your buyers.

Pond5 has a great keyword tool, that will recommend 20+ keywords to start with. I usually end up deleting some that I don't agree with but build on what they suggest. Then, I switch to text mode, copy and paste it into my spreadsheet, so it is available to copy to other similar clips. This all takes time but is worth every minute you invest.

Artificial Intelligence is here to stay, and what it can do is accelerating with incredible speed. At least in its current form, *there are proven examples of how it plagiarizes existing creative works*. At the time of this writing, the WGA, DGA and SAG unions are fighting to limit its use, and it's quite possible other types of limiting legislation are on their way. I would strongly advise caution if you are considering to use it to generate videos to upload as stock footage.

The stock agencies may develop and update policies on AI-generated content—I suggest keeping an eye on their shoot briefs, contributor portals, artist forums and policy pages to keep abreast of changes.

That said, AI can be an excellent research tool for coming up with keywords, titles and descriptions. Try especially searching for metaphors in the prompts. You will need to set up a free account at OpenAI.com. Then you can just type in a text message in the prompt and see what happens.

Here's a working example of using AI to help generate keywords. My highest selling clip is of a blue eye that has a pupil that dilates. What if I want to come up with metaphorical keywords?

First I type in: "metaphor keywords for blue eye with dilating pupil"

Result 1:

1. Oceanic depth
2. Enlarged curiosity
3. Sapphire intrigue
4. Amplified wonder
5. Expansive inquisitiveness
6. Dilating mystery
7. Deepening fascination
8. Augmented perception
9. Widened perception
10. Pupil-piercing insight

Though I could pull a few things from this list, like "widened" and "amplified," this is not quite what I was looking for.

My 2nd prompt focuses more on emotions: "metaphor emotion keywords for eye with dilating pupil" (note that I dropped "blue" because it wasn't relevant, and added "emotion")

Result 2:

1. Intense fascination
2. Overwhelming curiosity
3. Enchanted captivation
4. Awe-inspiring wonder
5. Spellbound enchantment
6. Pulsing excitement
7. Breathless anticipation
8. Throbbing intrigue
9. Heart-stopping amazement
10. Enraptured fascination
11. Hypnotic enthrallment
12. All-consuming interest
13. Unwavering attention
14. Rapturous captivation
15. Unbridled enthusiasm

Much closer! I realize now that the 2-word combinations are tripping me up. So this time I type in "Refine: single words"

Result 3:

1. Intrigue
2. Wonder
3. Curiosity
4. Intensity

5. Amazement
6. Fascination
7. Captivation
8. Astonishment
9. Anticipation
10. Excitement
11. Attraction
12. Engagement
13. Absorption
14. Attentiveness
15. Enchantment

This is getting there! I could pull a number of these, and could also continue to refine with negative emotions, etc. I'm on my way to much more diverse metaphorical keywords.

Now let's try to figure out some things that could help me describe it. My new prompt is "possible applications for video clip containing closeup of eye with pupil dilating."

Here is the result:

1. Film and TV: The video clip could be used in movies, TV shows, or commercials to convey different emotions like curiosity, intrigue, or surprise.

2. Education: The clip could be used in educational videos to illustrate the biology of the human eye and how it reacts to light and stimuli.

3. Psychology: The video clip could be used in psychology research to study the physiological and psychological responses to different stimuli.

4. Medical: The clip could be used in medical training to teach students how to perform eye exams and to identify changes in pupil size that could be indicative of different medical conditions.

5. Gaming: The video clip could be used in video games as a visual effect to represent different emotions or states of mind, like heightened awareness or concentration.

6. Art: The clip could be used in various forms of visual art to create abstract or surreal compositions that evoke different emotions or moods.

7. Marketing: The video clip could be used in advertising to create a sense of intrigue or interest in a product or service by associating it with the emotions conveyed by the dilating pupil.

These are actually quite helpful, particularly toward the end of each sentence! I can definitely pull from these for different ways of using the clip. *Note that I will rarely use the AI version as is. I use it to help get ideas, then pull from the result to put it into my own words.*

I will gather more AI strategies and post them at the website at http://sellstockebook.com. If you have your own, please share them with me via my Twitter @GrayJones and Instagram @grahamajones.

CHAPTER 13: CHOOSING THE RIGHT STOCK FOOTAGE AGENCY

In this chapter, we'll discuss how to select the right stock footage agency to maximize sales of your content. We'll also explore the pros and cons of becoming an exclusive contributor at one agency like Pond5 versus diversifying and selling at multiple agencies.

CHOOSING THE RIGHT STOCK FOOTAGE AGENCY

There are many stock footage agencies to choose from, and it can be overwhelming to decide which one to work with. Here are some factors to consider when choosing the right agency:

1. **Agency Reputation:** Research the agency's reputation and track record in the industry. Look for reviews and feedback from other contributors to gauge their experience working with the agency. The most reputable agencies at the moment are Pond5, Shutterstock, Adobe, and Envato.
2. **Commission Rates:** Check the commission rates offered by the agency. Some agencies may offer higher commission rates, but they may also have stricter content requirements. At the moment the only ones I would take seriously are Pond5 (60% commission if you're exclusive, 40% if you're non-exclusive), Adobe (33%), and Shutterstock (30%). Others are just too low

commission: Envato pays 20%, and iStock pays 20% for non-exclusive and a sliding scale for exclusive contributors up to 45%.

3. **Content Requirements:** Check the agency's content requirements to ensure your footage meets their standards. Some agencies may require higher resolution footage, specific formats, or have strict content guidelines. Some may accept audio clips or music, and others won't.

4. **Distribution Network:** Consider the agency's distribution network and how they market and promote their content to buyers. Some agencies may have a larger buyer base and more extensive marketing efforts, leading to higher sales potential. In particular, both Adobe and Pond5 offer a plugin to integrate with the Adobe Premiere editing program, so buyers can license footage right within the application. This definitely increases sales at these two agencies.

5. **Pricing:** Pond5 allows you precise control over the pricing. Others, like Shutterstock, don't. If you have highly specialized footage like military footage or my driving plates, this will be a deciding factor.

When it comes to selling stock footage, you have the option of going exclusive with one agency (at Pond5 or iStock) or diversifying and selling at multiple agencies. I used to sell at a number of agencies, and it worked for me for a long time, but it was also a ton of work to upload new material to all the different sites. When I saw sales fall off at Adobe and Shutterstock I decided to go all-in at Pond5 and enjoy their 60% commission for exclusive contributors. They also have fast approval times, high approval rates, and allow me to set my own prices. Also, exclusive contributors appear higher in search results, and get a special watermark on their thumbnails. And it is *so* much less work to upload to just one agency!

However, there are some downsides to exclusivity—it means limiting your reach to buyers who specifically use that agency. In particular, I know that Warner Bros is not allowed to use Pond5. I have heard of this being the case at some other companies, but for me, the benefits far outweigh these tradeoffs.

On the other hand, diversifying and selling at multiple agencies can offer broader exposure to a wider range of buyers. That being said, it can also mean more work in managing multiple accounts and adhering to different content requirements.

Ultimately, the decision to go exclusive or diversify depends on your goals and preferences. If you prioritize higher commission rates and are willing to limit your reach a little, or are concerned about streamlining your time, going exclusive at Pond5 may be the best option. If you prioritize broader exposure and are willing to put in the work to manage multiple accounts, diversifying may be a better fit.

What I suggest to my friends is to go exclusive at Pond5. But if they want to diversify, they can upload to the top 3 sites, and give it a few months. See if uploading to all three is manageable, and see which start to sell. If you find it's too much work, or Pond5 is the clear winner, then you can go exclusive at that point.

If you do upload to multiple sites, I suggest the tracking app MicroStockr: it's amazing to track your sales across the different sites and compare them. It also generates graphs and reports as well as shows you which are your top selling clips. If you're exclusive at Pond5, you can get all this info inside their dashboard.

You can find handy links on this book's website to sign up for the various stock footage agencies: sellstockebook.com/agencies.

Please mention "GrayJones" as referrer as you sign up. I will get a small affiliate commission, that does not affect how much you will earn. And you can do this too! More on this later.

THE APPLICATION PROCESS

The application process differs slightly at the different sites, but typically you choose your 10 best shots (try to have them be different in content and nature), prepare all their titles, descriptions and keywords, and then submit them for review. Within a few days or weeks, they will tell you if they approve your account, plus these first 10 clips will be ready for sale. Then, you can start uploading more!

CHAPTER 14: MARKETING YOUR STOCK FOOTAGE

In this chapter, we'll discuss how to effectively market your stock footage to potential buyers. We'll cover topics like building a website, using social media, and posting samples on YouTube while protecting your work from theft.

BUILDING A WEBSITE

Having a website dedicated to showcasing and selling your stock footage is an excellent way to market your work. This is especially important if you want to try to also use it as a platform to get hired for work in your area (for instance, for a drone business).

Try to register a catchy but short and simple name, preferably a ".com" address. If you use GoDaddy to host your site, you can use their free web builder to create a simple site or pay for premium features (this book's website was registered through GoDaddy and used their web builder). Be aware that if you want to attach the website to your own custom domain (highly recommended), you will have to upgrade and pay a monthly fee. You can also use website builders like Squarespace or Wix to create a professional-looking site that is easy to navigate and showcases your work in an organized manner. Wordpress is free and quite easy to learn if you don't mind doing some of the steps manually.

Once you have shot a decent number of clips, I would highly recommend editing a video of your best shots and making it available to play on your site (even auto-play). Make sure your website has a clear call-to-action to purchase your footage, and it's easy for buyers to find the content they need. You may have different buttons to go directly to different collections, for example. Additionally, consider offering a free sample clip or two to attract buyers to your site and encourage them to make a purchase.

USING SOCIAL MEDIA

Social media platforms like Twitter, Instagram, and Facebook can also be effective marketing tools for your stock footage. I've gotten *very* large contracts directly from social networks!

Make sure to include links to your website and highlight your new uploads whenever they are approved. *Remember that views of your videos make them appear higher on search results... It's not always about the immediate sales.*

Once you've built a bigger library, especially if you have a niche specialty, you might consider running paid social media ads to reach a broader audience and target buyers who may be interested in your content.

GET BUSINESS CARDS

Depending on your specialty, it may be a good idea to get business cards. This is especially important for drone shooters and wedding/event shooters. You never know when you will meet a potential client or even someone who knows a potential client! I will also put promos like my 10% referral deal right on the business card.

REAL LIFE NETWORKING

Look for opportunities for real life networking. We've gotten a lot of great leads at Comic-Con conventions, through our local church, and people we meet while hiking or shopping. Spread the word that you can do videos, and you'd be surprised who comes calling.

POSTING SAMPLES ON YOUTUBE

A lot of people don't make the connection that Google owns YouTube. I have found time and time again, that when I post videos on YouTube, I appear higher in the Google search results. As a result, I highly recommend posting samples of your stock footage on YouTube in order to showcase your work to potential buyers. I suggest editing together compilation videos with only the best parts of your best clips. However, it's crucial to protect your content from theft by watermarking your videos with your name or logo.

Make sure to include a call-to-action to visit your website or purchase the full clip in the video's description box. Additionally, consider creating tutorials or behind-the-scenes videos of your work to engage potential buyers and showcase your skills. Make sure they also know how to contact you for custom shooting—I've gotten several jobs this way.

Most of the stock footage sites have some kind of "affiliate of" referral program to help attract more contributors to the site. If I invite you to contribute, you get the exact same percentage of each sale, but I also receive a small percentage of that sale for a limited time as a referral bonus. It's a "win-win" for both of us, with no downside (Please mention "GrayJones" as referrer if you sign up for Pond5 or any of the other sites).

CHAPTER 15: MEET ALICIA & KEN

I really want to make sure you can clearly understand the process, so in this chapter we'll look at two fictional case studies (pieces of which are based on real people I've helped).

FICTIONAL CASE STUDY 1 - ALICIA

Alicia is an aspiring TV writer who recently graduated from USC. She grew up on a farm and is an extremely hard worker: she did two internships while in school and was an office production assistant in her first summer after she graduated, but she's currently in-between jobs. She's writing scripts and meeting regularly with a writers' group she joined in school, but she heard on the "Happier in Hollywood" podcast that even working writers often need some kind of side hustle. She happened to catch my blog post after watching one of my podcasts and thought she would give stock footage a try.

She grew up in the age of the smartphone and has taken years of video, so she starts there. One Saturday she buckles down and sifts her Photos app to show only videos. She creates albums for Good, Great, and Awesome, and starts going through the footage.

It takes way longer than she thought, but she's excited to find at least 50 awesome videos from what she shot, and perhaps another 50 in the Great album.

She decides on an aggressive plan... by hook or by crook, she's going to upload 10/day until she gets a job, and 5/day after that. She picks her 10 best and submits them to Pond5. She opts for the Exclusive program, because she likes the 60% commission and other perks like appearing higher in searches, and she's concerned it will be too much work to upload to several sites if she gets busy. To stretch out her older videos, she decides that she'll challenge herself to get at least one new shot wherever she goes. She's approved quickly and decided to start shooting!

While she's waiting for the bus, she crouches down and captures feet walking past. When she meets with her writing group, she gets closeups of fingers tapping on the keyboard, of Final Draft script lines being typed in, hands writing notes on paper. She grabs a coffee and realizes she can capture a cool shot of the barista fixing the drink, all without showing any logos or faces. Suddenly this becomes a game for her, and by the end of the day she realizes she has 15 great shots and didn't have to pull from her old videos. Of course she's a writer, so she has no problem doing great titles, descriptions and keywords.

She keeps on like this, getting 15-20 clips a day. Pretty soon she realizes that everywhere she goes she's capturing stock footage, so she can write a lot of expenses off!

After 2 or 3 weeks and a couple hundred clips submitted, she finally gets her first sale! She celebrates, but reminds herself that sales will be slow in the beginning. So she keeps at it.

Alicia shoots all the things she can think of at home, but she eventually starts to run out of ideas. Now, she starts researching things in her area she can capture. She goes to a street festival and gets tons of shots, then to a flea market, and an outdoor concert. Because she's been challenging herself so much, she's a natural now at finding closeups, shots that express a metaphor, and some good editorial shots of crowds. She also finds a lot of people are happy to sign releases, and she gets tons of great shots of diverse people together. She has so much great footage that it will take her weeks to go through it all... which is great because she just landed another assistant job.

Because she has all the festival footage and her older videos, she decides to challenge herself and keep her daily upload to 10/day. Between work in the day and uploading at night, she barely has time to check her email. A few months in, she comes in to work and finds out the show has been cancelled.

Regrouping, she logs in to Pond5... and discovers that she has passed 2,000 uploaded clips! There's a notification that she needs to set up PayPal so she can get paid... and there's $4,500 to deposit.

OK, I took some liberties here... she would know earlier that she was having sales. But if you put your mind to it and always look for opportunities, it is absolutely possible to build a library that quickly, especially if you are between jobs. Let's continue Alicia's story...

Alicia decides that with no job, she's going to keep costs low and keep shooting with her phone. But she invests in a used tripod and the newest DJI phone gimbal to up her game. Bolstered by her sales, she plans further and further trips away, goes home to visit her family and shoots while she's there, and continues daily to add to her catalog.

By the end of the first year, she's at 5,000 clips and $5,000/month revenue. But she's a woman on a mission, and decides that no matter what, she's going to reach 10,000 clips by the end of her 2nd year. She continues to add 10-12 clips/day, while writing, networking, getting with her writing group and applying for jobs. She lands a writer's assistant job during that second year but still manages to keep up the pace, uploading in the evenings when her day is done.

By the end of that 2nd year, she makes it! Her library has 10,000 clips. She has told herself that she will stop completely when she gets her first staff job… and the call happens to come on that day. She laughs, as she realizes she's making more monthly from her stock footage than the job is paying her. To celebrate, she turns on the TV… and sees one of her stock footage clips in a commercial.

Alicia is never going to have to worry if she gets fired, if the writers go on strike, or she has too long of a gap between jobs. She can take whatever time she needs off to develop her own shows, and never worry about her rent being paid.

And outside of that first weekend sifting through old videos, during this two year time, she never worked more than 40 minutes in a day. Slow but steady wins the race!

Ken is a different case... his story is more directly related to actual events.

"Ken" was a middle-aged reality TV editor I worked with. He heard that my driving plates were used in the "Hollywood Puppet Show" television series, and wanted to know more about selling stock footage.

As I talked with him, I learned that his family had gone on a ton of road and air trips growing up, and that they were constantly rolling their video tape camcorder. They had gone to major landmarks, national parks, air and space museums... and he continued the tradition shooting lots of footage with his own family. Because his dad worked in the military, he had shot some amazing footage of helicopters, planes and other stuff around the bases. Thankfully, his whole family was still alive, so he got release forms from all of them.

He was eager to try uploading to several of the big sites, but I expressed a concern that the military footage should be sold on Pond5, where he could control the pricing. So he set up one exclusive account on Pond5 that was for all his military footage, and then another general account that he would upload the historical footage.

Because of the volume of tapes he had, it was going to be a ton of work. It would be way too expensive to get a service to import his videotapes, so he set aside some down time between jobs to rent the equipment to do it himself. This would include a Teranex (a device that intelligently up-converts to 1080p or 4K in real time) because he knew it would sell better on the stock sites if it was up-converted to a higher resolution.

He ended up with so much historical footage that it made more sense to send a hard drive to the stock footage sites instead of uploading.

Largely because of the military footage, he got $1,000 of sales in his first month! It was a wise strategy to have a second account and control the pricing. And because he had such a large volume of historical footage in different locations, his sales continued to grow rapidly from there.

Ken got busy, and still has a ton of footage to wade through. Every time he has a break between jobs he's going to work on posting more of the footage. But receiving a few thousand extra dollars every month sure takes the edge off!

Different Stories, Different Strategies

Alicia and Ken's stories couldn't be more different. They each assessed what they brought to the table and played to their strengths. Not everyone can upload 10-12/day. Not everyone is sitting on a ton of older videos. But there is a strategy that will work with you and your schedule.

I do think that Alicia's spirit, trying to look for opportunities in daily life and making a game of it, is an attitude very well suited to capturing on a smartphone. Keeping her costs low was also a great idea.

SUMMARY

In this chapter, we heard two mostly fictional stories, about Alicia and Ken. They each brought very different things to the table, but each were able to find an effective strategy to build a strong passive income through different types of stock footage.

What will your strategy be?

I'm happy to hear your strategies, and feel free to tweet them to me at @GrayJones or send them via Instagram at @grahamajones. I've helped many people develop solid passive incomes, and I'd be glad to help you too!

CHAPTER 16: CONCLUSION

Did we accomplish our objective? Are you now able to build a six figure yearly passive income with only the phone in your pocket?

RECAP OF KEY POINTS

- **In Chapter 1**, we defined what stock footage is, why it remains in demand, and who the buyers are, as well as how it is continually evolving based on technical advances and new trends, which continually create new opportunities. A key take-away is that Pond5's catalog contains only 0.6% vertical video, and Adobe is actively asking for more.
- **In Chapter 2,** we discussed the power of passive income, and how once you plant the seeds of stock footage they continue to grow without intervention, even when you're not adding more material. We also learned about the tremendous tax benefits, and money you can save through writing off business expenses.
- **In Chapter 3,** we covered how to get started: looking around you at what's available to you. We talked about technical considerations for using phones, starting with what you have. We also discussed resolution, frame rate, editing software, when you might want to upgrade to an interchangeable lens camera, and what you might need if you do.
- **In Chapter 4,** we discussed how to research the catalogs of the different stock agencies, to look

for opportunities. We also discussed picking a niche or specialty, or how you can use collections if you want to shoot in multiple niches.

- **In Chapter 5,** we talked about ways of moving the camera, as well as moving the subject. We also discussed being a student of behind-the-scenes videos, always looking for creative ideas, and keeping an idea journal/look book.

- **In Chapter 6,** we went deeper into what to shoot, trying to approach it from the perspective of the buyer and what they're looking for. We used James Orlowski's catalog as a case study on how to express metaphors in what we shoot. We also looked at the contributor resources on some of the main sites as well as strategies on consistently building your library, including ideas on planning ahead to events and holidays.

- **In Chapter 7,** we discussed still photography, and looked at opportunities to create graphic content right from your computer, like CGI, effects, background templates, 3D models, and animations.

- **In Chapter 8,** we had a brief look at resources available if you're interested in recording sound effects. We also examined possibilities for existing musicians to approach licensing your music.

- **In Chapter 9,** we covered many pricing strategies, including temporarily dropping your prices to attract views and sales, but making sure not to chase the bottom. We covered free clip promotions, subscription sales, credit packs, and how to approach regular pricing of your clips for greatest perceived value.

- **In Chapter 10,** we looked at the legal side, with trademarks, model and property releases, Greeking a location, and editorial-only content.
- **In Chapter 11,** we learned how to select the best clips, and how to organize and name them, as well as the importance of using high quality hard drives and maintaining backups.
- **In Chapter 12,** we covered what could be the most important part—how the buyer will find the clip, via the title, description, and keywords. We discussed SEO strategies and an intro to using AI to help with this part of the process.
- **In Chapter 13,** we addressed how to choose the right stock agency, and whether you should go exclusive or diversify, plus a strategy of starting with 3 sites and re-evaluating later. We also addressed what the application process would look like.
- **In Chapter 14,** we talked about different ways to market your stock footage, by building a website, using social networks, having business cards, networking in real life, and posting samples on YouTube. We also discussed other ways of earning money, through clients hiring you because of what they see in your footage, and also how to make some money through affiliate programs.
- **In Chapter 15,** we met Alicia and Ken, and heard two mostly fictional case studies that were able to find a strategy that worked for them despite coming from two very different lives.

Stock footage is not a "get rich scheme." If anything, it's "get rich slow." Slow but steady will win this particular race. I believe that because of smartphone shooting, vertical video, new tools, and an ever-expanding number of content creators who need to buy it, this field is ripe with new opportunity.

Even so, in my own life and the people I've helped, I have observed that it almost always takes several months before your first sale, and sales are usually slow in the beginning. This is partly because other people's clips with more views and sales appear higher than yours, and in part because there's always a learning curve to capturing the metaphor instead of the pretty shot.

It's extremely tempting to give up when you don't see results. However, if you want to succeed in stock footage, you need to think like a farmer: the more seeds you plant, the more fruit you'll have. It really is that simple.

You have to play smart, being a student of trends and thinking metaphorically, but ultimately it comes down to consistently doing the work: planting more and more seeds and "watering" them by researching trends and promoting through social networks, websites, and other ways we discussed.

Will you reach $100,000/year with 6,200 clips, like James did? Will it take 7,000 clips? Or 8,000 clips? It doesn't really matter, because if you just focus on adding more and more, eventually the sales will come.

I think a good rule of thumb is that the average shot that is well captured (according to what I've shown you) will generate $10/year. That may not sound like much, but keep in mind that it will continue to sell over the next 20 years. If you have a library of 100 clips, that will generate $20,000 over the next 20 years. A library of 1,000 clips will generate $200,000. A library of 10,000 clips will generate $2 million.

Of course these are simplifications, but you can use $10/clip/year as a way of figuring out how much to shoot to achieve your desired goals.

Don't forget that you don't jump from 0 to $100K overnight! You will start with a $500 month, then a $1,000 month, and then a $2,000 month. Pretty soon you'll have a $3,000 month, and then a $5,000 month. And maybe when you reach $10,000/month you keep going!

For me, visualizing the end goal helps motivate me in the present. Imagine if 5 years from now, through nothing but the phone in your pocket, you no longer had to work or think about money, and all your needs and your family's needs were taken care of. What is that worth to you?

Now... what will you do to get it?

APPENDIX 1: RESOURCES AND TOOLS

One of the things that most quickly dates a book is when an author lists current models of cameras or versions of software. Even the stock footage agencies come and go... several sites that gave me a lot of sales don't exist any more.

As a result, please visit and bookmark the book's website http://sellstockebook.com, as I will keep that updated with lots of information on recommended equipment, agency links, software, books, AI updates, and other tips and tricks.

Follow me on Twitter at @GrayJones, and on Instagram at @grahamajones. I respond to messages on both those platforms very quickly, usually within 24 hours. Even better, tag me whenever you get a sale, and I'll retweet it, helping your clip get more views!

Twitter Tip: never start a tweet with '@' if you want it to be public. The @ symbol limits who sees the tweet to the person you are tagging any anyone who follows BOTH you and them. The solution: put a preceding period. So the tweet might look like ".@GrayJones look what I just sold!"

You can also send me a personal email at grayjonesmail@gmail.com. I'd love to hear your comments, compliments, and suggestions, and I'm happy to answer any questions you have.

APPENDIX 2: GLOSSARY OF COMMON TERMS IN STOCK FOOTAGE INDUSTRY

- **3D models:** Computer-generated 3D objects that can be used in films and videos to create realistic environments and special effects.
- **4K resolution:** A video format that provides four times the resolution of standard high-definition video.
- **B-roll:** Additional footage used to complement or support the main footage (A-roll).
- **Camera Pan:** Moving the camera horizontally to follow the action or reveal a new subject or setting.
- **Camera tilt:** A shot in which the camera moves up or down, pivoting on a fixed point, to capture a scene or subject from a different angle.
- **CGI (Computer-Generated Imagery):** The use of computer graphics to create visual effects and animations.
- **Cutaway:** A shot that interrupts the main scene to show something else, such as a close-up of an object or a person's reaction.
- **Establishing shot:** A wide-angle shot used at the beginning of a scene to establish the location or setting.
- **Footage:** The raw, unedited material that has been captured on film or video.
- **Foley:** The reproduction of everyday sound effects that are added to film and video to enhance audio quality.
- **Frame rate:** The number of individual frames that are captured per second.

- **High-definition (HD):** A video format that provides a higher resolution and image quality than standard-definition video.

- **Long shot (LS):** A shot that shows the subject from a distance, typically to establish the location or setting.

- **Music:** Compositions that are created and added to film and video to enhance the emotional impact of the production.

- **Scenics:** A type of B-roll that is categorized by wider shots of scenery. This can be urban or rural.

- **Slow motion:** Capturing video at a higher frame rate than the standard frame rate and then slowing it down to create a slow-motion effect.

- **Sound effects:** Audio elements that are added to film and video to create a sense of realism and enhance the viewer's experience.

- **Still photography:** Photographs taken with a still camera that can be used as stock images in films, TV shows, or commercials.

- **Teranex:** A device that intelligently compares adjacent frames to rebuild missing information as it deinterlaces and upscales footage to higher resolution.

- **Time-lapse:** Capturing video over an extended period and then playing it back at a faster rate to create an effect that suggests a quick passage of time.

- **Tracking shot:** A shot that follows a subject as it moves through the scene, typically using a dolly or steadicam.

- **Zoom:** Changing the focal length of the lens to make the subject appear closer or further away.

APPENDIX 3: FAQ

Here are some questions I've been asked about the process of selling stock footage.

Q: I've uploaded a lot... why am I not seeing many sales?
A: This is a very common question. Sometimes it is simply that your footage has not had the views and sales yet, so is appearing lower on searches. Other times, it's because you're aiming at niches that are too saturated, or you have too many pretty shots and not enough specificity and/or metaphors. It can also be that you're not putting enough thought into the title, description and keywords. As you go, you may want to revisit some of the chapters of this book.

Q: What are some common mistakes?
A: By far, the most common mistake is thinking the pretty shot will sell, and not going after specificity, either of metaphor or of location. The 2nd most common mistake is giving up too early. I barely had any sales my first year, but since then have grown my library to the point where I have months where I earn $10,000.

Q: I'm a cinematographer. Won't this dilute my brand?
A: I hear this a lot! I would say, take a page from Apple Computer. You can buy an iPad at Walmart or Costco, but you will never mistake that you're buying a premium product, because of how it's priced. There are indeed stock footage sites like FilmSupply that

cater to high end cinematographers, but you can also accomplish the same thing on a site like Pond5 by:

1. going exclusive,
2. setting up your profile as a premium brand, and
3. pricing your clips very high, from $199-$499.

For instance, I set up my @DrivingFootage as a premium brand, and no clip is priced below $179.

Q: Why do I have some very slow months?
A: Stock footage is very seasonal, and there are big ebbs and flows. Of course there are the holidays and literal seasons, but it can also be motivated by the news and other trends. I will have some months I only get $230, others $1,350, and sometimes $10,000. And there is no rhyme or reason… I have had $760 of sales on a single Sunday during Christmas holidays: at that time, most media companies are shut down. Diversifying your catalog and being prepared for the various seasons and holidays will help to stabilize the big ups and downs.

Q: What about other stock footage agencies not mentioned here?
A: There are indeed many others… some, I don't mention because I've had bad experiences with them; others, because they generated almost zero sales; still

others, because I had no personal experience with them. You are welcome to try, but I would concentrate on the most well-known agencies.

Q: I love still photography and have many amazing shots. Can I sell those too?
A: Absolutely, there is still a market for photos, though it is much more competitive and saturated. You may make as low as $1 on each download depending on the resolution, but you can get a lot higher quantity of downloads. I would say make this a lower priority than your videos, but if you run out of videos to upload, you can try uploading stills.

Q: Many of my videos are 1080p, 720p or even standard definition. Can I sell these too?
A: As of right now, stock footage sites are less interested in resolutions under 1080p, so standard definition would have to be of special interest (for instance footage of a protest, political event, historical interest, or something like that). 1080p is still selling very well, but it prices a little over 50% of what 4K sells for, so you won't earn as much per sale. I would make your 4K material your highest priority, and if you run out of 4K, then start uploading your lower resolution footage.

Q: How often will I get paid?
A: It works in much the same way as YouTube or Amazon affiliate income. If you pass a certain threshold of sales, you will be paid once per month. For Pond5, it's on the 15th.

Q: Why do I sometimes get a $10 or $3 sale?
A: The stock agencies have different ways of selling your clip. Firstly, even if your clip is 4K, they will sell lower resolution versions for lower prices. Secondly, they may sell via subscriptions or credit packs, which pay far less per sale to the artist. I strongly advise against opting in to subscriptions and credit packs, but if a low resolution version of the clip sells for $10 I still celebrate, because that clip will now appear much higher in searches.

Q: How much should I set aside for taxes?
A: It depends on a lot of things... how you set up your business, how many deductions you have, what country you're in. Treat it as any non-employment income would be (for instance, like contract work). I do recommend setting it up as a bona fide home business, so you can write off expenses like a gimbal, tripod, jib, and part of your phone bill against your income.

Q: How is my privacy protected?

A: The stock footage agencies build their business on licensing content within set terms. They are constantly hunting the web for violators. As for your own info, you can choose whatever info you wish to display. Generally it is good to mention your city (because some of your footage may be particular to your location), but you can choose a pseudonym, and have any info you like on your public profile.

Feel free to ask me any other questions on Twitter at @GrayJones or Instagram @GrahamAJones. Also check the website at http://sellstockebook.com for more information and a more regularly updated FAQ.

About the Author

Recently featured on the popular Side Hustle School podcast, in an episode entitled 'Hollywood Editor Shoots for the Stars.' Also featured on 'Fitness in Post,' 'Screenwriters' Rant Room' and 'Show Don't Tell' podcasts.

With over 325 TV & film credits and at least 5 development projects picked up to series, **Gray Jones** is a TV editor, produced writer, author, entrepreneur and seminar leader located in LA. His extensive experience in many disciplines and genres gives him a unique blend of speed, story skills and graphics ability.

He has a very interesting history: high school class president; released an album in 1990 and toured Canada with his rock band; was a Christian minister for 6 years; won awards internationally for a short film he produced and shot; released a software program that was featured in Macworld Magazine; and has worked in TV series editing since 2001.

Gray is a world-renowned podcast producer and host. In January, 2008, he started "Chuck vs. the Podcast" for NBC's Chuck, which was voted the world's #1 TV-themed podcast for 40 consecutive months. He was featured on CNN and in the Toronto Star for the key role he played in the successful fan renewal campaigns. Over its 107 episode run, the podcast featured over 160 interviews with the cast, crew, and writers of the show.

In 2010, Gray partnered with Script Magazine to launch the "TV Writer Podcast," a video podcast dedicated to interviews with working writers. Since its launch in August, 2010, Gray has interviewed over 130 show creators, show runners, writers, and authors from Hollywood, Canada, and the UK.

After moderating a panel called "How to Write a TV Pilot" at San Diego Comic-Con in 2014, Gray published his first book, "How To Break In To TV Writing: Insider Interviews."

In 2015, Gray and his wife Sherrey Lee Jones launched a YouTube channel for kids, called "ABC123Songs." In addition to producing and performing and all the music, as well as production, cinematography and directing for the green screen shoots, Gray did all the animation and editing. He also narrated dozens of Read Along Stories for the channel.

In 2018, Gray launched drivingfootage.com, a website selling 9-angle driving plates for film & TV, shot with his custom-designed height adjustable driving plates rig. As of May 2023, he has over 14,000 4K clips available for sale, and is shooting more all the time. He also rents out a wide variety of production and post gear, specializing in micro four thirds cameras and vintage decks, through the ShareGrid sharing site.

Most recently, Gray formed a company called Archive2Digital.com, specializing in high volume, high speed importing and restoration of video tapes and films. Clients have included Maroon 5, Bunim Murray, the late Betty White, the Sea Shepherd organization, the Grateful Dead, and the Milken Family Foundation.

As evidenced by his podcast work, Gray loves to give back. He often volunteers his time for charity work, as well as educates via his seminars and webinars for Moviola Learning, BorisFX, and on his own YouTube channel. He has had guest appearances on several podcasts and radio & TV shows over the years: Gray was recently interviewed for a documentary on fan campaigns called United We Fan (available on Amazon Prime).

Originally from Canada, he has an honors BFA in Film & TV Screenwriting and Production from York University, where he graduated with distinction in 1994.

Gray is proud to put family and spiritual values first, and strives always to produce material that will help people in some way.

ONE LAST THING...

If you enjoyed this book or found it useful, I'd be very grateful if you'd post a short review on Amazon. Your support really does make a difference: I read all the reviews personally so I can get your feedback and make this book even better.

If you'd like to leave a review then all you need to do is click the review link on this book's page on Amazon.

Thanks so much!

Made in the USA
Monee, IL
22 June 2023

35915216R00066